The Complete Gambling Playbook

Amogelang Mkhonza

Published by Amogelang Mkhonza, 2025.

THE COMPLETE GAMBLING PLAYBOOK

First edition. March 21, 2025.

ISBN: 979-8230038672

Written by Amogelang Mkhonza.

GAMBLING IS NOT REALLY about how well you play the games, it's about how you handle your money. - V.P Pappy

Discover The Complete Gambling Playbook—a game-changing guide blending luck with strategy. Packed with insider tips, proven methods, and captivating stories. It equips you with all the tools to master smart gambling. Whether you're a rookie or experienced gambler. This playbook is also your blueprint for rewriting- The rules of the game and seizing control of your destiny. A journey to smart gambling, where timeless wisdom-meets cutting edge strategies in a heart-compounding world.

2

UPDATED EDITION ENHANCED WITH PERSONAL STORIES, REAL-WORLD EXAMPLES & PRACTICAL INSIGHTS

CONTENTS

The Complete Gambling Playbook

INTRODUCTION

A Global Phenomenon (History & Evolution)

IN A WORLD PULSATING with excitement and the lure of fortune, the thrill of gambling has captured the hearts of countless individuals (including me).

Whether it's the spin of a roulette wheel, the flip of a card, the roll of a dice, or the high-stakes of a parlay, the tension of a poker hand , the thrill of a slot machine spinning ,the anticipation of a bingo draw, or the hope of hitting it big on a lottery ticket and that's just the beginning, countless other games are out there, each offering its own excitement and reward, all from the vibrant casino floors, race tracks and Ekasi street dice games to the convenience of online platforms and many other spots where bets are placed, the world of gambling has something for everyone.

Gambling is universally captivating because of its blend of chance, skill and the potential of a great reward. It can evoke a sense of adrenaline that is almost impossible to replicate in any other domain. It's a total mind-fuck. From the unassuming local bettors to the seasoned professional gamblers, everyone is drawn to the allure of risking something for the possibility of a win—sometimes life-changing

The roots of gambling stretch back thousands of years, early records show that humans have always had a fascination with games of chance, and these pursuits were intertwined with cultural rituals and celebrations, oh even religious practices—now calm down amigo, before you start clutching your pearls, getting all worked up, and calling me a liar. In many cultures throughout history, gambling was not solely seen as a form of entertainment but it could have been used as a part of rituals to seek divine favor, predict the future, or as a symbolic act during religious festivals or gatherings. The Ancient Roman and Greek cultures often used dice in religious rituals, where casting lots was believed to communicate with the gods or decide important matters, with outcomes believed to be guided by high powers. So, gambling was sometimes more than just a game; it was part of a larger spiritual or religious context.

The ancient Chinese, for example, were playing Keno as early as 2000 BCE, while the Greeks and Romans incorporated betting and gambling into their social fabric, with gladiator games and chariot races that were not only for spectacles but also opportunities for wagers. Fast forward to the Middle Ages, gambling became popular in royal courts, with card and dice games enjoyed by nobility. During the Renaissance, gambling not only served as entertainment but also a tool for political power, with rulers using it to raise funds for wars.

In the 19th century, modern gambling began to take shape, especially with the rise of organized casinos. The invention of the slot machine by Charles Fey in 1895 revolutionized the industry, and cities like Las Vegas became hubs for casino culture. In the U.S gambling grew during the Gold Rush and frontier days, while legal frameworks began to form, though the practice remained largely unregulated in many places.

The 20th century then now saw gambling reach mainstream popularity, particularly after Nevada legalized casinos in 1931, making Las Vegas a global symbol of the industry. Online gambling was then introduced in the late

1990s, following the legalization of online gaming by Antigua and Barbuda, it marked a significant shift, expanding gambling to global audiences via the innanet.

In the 21st century, the industry underwent digital transformation, with online gambling growing into a multi-billion-dollar business. The rise of mobile technology allowed for on-the-go betting, while live dealer games brought a more authentic casino experience to homes. E-sports betting and fantasy sports also gained popularity, attracting younger demographic. Cryptocurrencies like Bitcoin entered the scene, providing a more anonymous and decentralized way to gamble, I know you probably don't get this, it's okay ska wara that's why I'm here, let me break this down for you, cryptocurrencies allow users to make transaction that don't require personal information. This makes it harder to track identities of users involved in gambling, which appeals to those who value privacy. Cryptocurrencies operate on decentralized networks, meaning no central authority like banks or any other third party oversees the transactions, allowing for more privacy and independence.

Despite its long history, gambling has faced moral scrutiny and regulations from governments and religious groups. However, it continues to thrive, with tighter global regulations aimed at ensuring consumer protection. Today, is not just about the games and money, well for me it is but that's not the point, the point is gambling is a global cultural phenomenon with an ever-expanding digital presence and an immense economic impact.

With all that being said, gambling has evolved from a social pastime to a multifaceted global industry, adapting to cultural shifts, technological advancement, and changing regulations.

Yet as enticing as the world of gambling may be, it is not without its perils. Now hear me out.

The Fine Line: Fun or Folly?

Archie Karas was flat-broke. Not the "I-can't-a-afford-a-hennessy" kind of broke. The "I-have-no-job, no prospects" kind of broke. Archie landed in Vegas in December 1992 with only $50 in his pocket and no real plan except to gamble, like a kid walking into a store a store with enough money for a single lollipop, but dreaming of a whole sugar rush and more snacks. But this wasn't some guy throwing dice with his last few bucks in the casino. This was the guy with the kind of audacity that only someone who has nothing to lose could have. Archie wasn't just playing and betting on poker, he had nothing but was betting everything—his luck, his skill, his nerve—against the house that held all the cards. And oh boy for a while, it worked. Like really worked.

Long story short, over a three-year span Archie won as much as $40 million from the $50 he started with. It was a legendary Las Vegas hot streak in the 1990. He became famous for "The run', which has been referred to as the biggest gambling winning streak in recorded history.

It wasn't some slow-and-steady climb. It was the kind of stuff you see in movies. Archie started at the low-stakes poker tables, sharpening his skills. One night at a poker table he managed to turn a few hundred into a few thousands, then the other nights a few thousands into a few hundred thousand, so on and so on. Poker wasn't enough for Archie, so he upped the ante, he hit the blackjack tables.

He wasn't just playing for small pots, he was throwing down tens of thousands of dollars per hand—insane stakes, insane confidence. And somehow it kept paying off. He had the perfect combination of nerve and luck. Every hand, every roll of the dice, every card that fell his way someway somehow seemed to come up in his favor. Saying Archie was on fire is even an understatement. He wasn't the guy sitting at a poker table, he was the show. He would walk into any casino and play with the highest rollers, winning more and more, all while his money kept piling up.

After three years of playing, Archie Karas was sitting on $40 million. That's $40 million made from pure, unrelenting risk and an incredible run of good fortune. His name was on everyone's lips. Archie was a myth, a man who had defied the odds in a way that no one thought possible. Casinos that once treated him as a nobody were now begging him to stay and play. It's a pity Snowfall wasn't released at the time, he would've been on that Franklin Saint's "I buuuilt this shit, ME! brick by brick ".

But here's a kicker. When you win big, there's a kind of addictive rush that comes with it. You're on top, you've beaten the system, and obviously as delusion as a human brain can sometimes you start thinking you can't lose. For someone like Archie $40 million wasn't enough. He's forgotten what it was like to start with $50 and a prayer. Now, he's so far removed from that struggle, all he sees is more zeros. Funny how the more you get, the less you appreciate, despite all of our sweat, struggle and strain we end up feeling similar to how we started: inadequate, it's a hedonic treadmill. Well, next time you are at a party and want to impress someone, try dropping that concept on them.

$40 million wasn't enough for Archie. In fact, it started to feel too safe. So, the guy kept placing bigger bets. He went from tables in baccarat and craps—games with enormous swings and absurdly high risks. At first it was still fun. Archie was living the dream, rolling the dice with millions of dollars at stake. Every win was a little more fun than the last, he was gambling to feel that electricity in his veins. And every time he won, it only got better. Every game felt like it was made for him. It wasn't just a game—it was his game, his world, his rules and no one could touch him. The adrenaline was there, but with every bet, the stakes were getting higher. He was no longer just a millionaire gambler having fun, he was a high-stakes thrill-seeker addicted to the chaos I'd say. His losses started to come in faster than he was used to. Now me and you we'd stop right and stay with what we have left right? I mean it's enough after all. But Archie didn't slow down. He kept doubling down, convinced that his luck would swing back his way. The problem? it didn't.

The house always has the edge, and sooner or later, that edge catches up with even the most brilliant gamblers. The bets became astronomical, every bet was like a dare to the universe, "Come on, I've beaten the odds for months, why not one more?" he thought. And that's where it shifted from fun to folly. He started losing BIG—too big to handle. His $40 million, the fortune he had built from nothing, was now evaporating at lightning speed. Archie wasn't just gambling now; he was chasing the high from his previous wins, desperately trying to get back to the top. It was no longer fun—it was reckless. And before he knew it, the house that once feared him was now laughing at his losses.

Archie kept losing, until it was all gone. Every dollar, every chip. $40 million wiped out in a series of reckless bets, bad decisions, and a belief that the streak could never end.

The line between fun and folly is razor-thin. When you're winning, it feels like the world is yours. But the moment you start chasing that rush, you're no longer playing the game—you're letting the game play you. In those early days, Archie's story was pure fun, it was the kind of wild, impossible that makes the legends. His meteoric rise was a testament to his skills and audacity. But somewhere along the way, it crossed over into folly. What starts as a shot at greatness, can easily turn into an obsession. He ignored the simple truth of gambling: eventually, the odds will catch up to you.

In hindsight, Archie's story highlights the delicate balance between risk and reward, while it can be fun and profitable in the short term, the sheer unpredictability and risk involved make it a dangerous pursuit, especially when one loses sight of the bigger picture.

Gambling is meant to be a form of entertainment, a way to have fun with money you can afford to lose, it's about enjoying the game. It's not meant to be a high or crutch. If you overdo it, it can become a dopamine chase, turning into an addictive cycle. In the next chapter, we'll dive deeper into how dopamine plays a role in this and why it can lead to compulsive behavior.

Gambling Dopamine Is Overrated

Dopamine—the brain's little "feel-good" chemical, like the high-five your brain gives itself when you do something pleasurable. And gambling? It's a dopamine rollercoaster. But the thing is gambling's dopamine rush is overrated. Like, way overrated. It's a cheap thrill that's about as satisfying as ordering an Uber for a two-minute ride to the corner store (Didn't know what example to use, ke motho lenna ka lapa).

The fun it's in the before—that sweet, sneaky little moment when you haven't even placed the bet, spun the slot machine or thrown the dice yet, but your brain is already throwing a party. Your heart starts racing with Max Verstappen, you feel the rush of possibility, and you're already imagining the celebrations. Dopamine is flooding your system, all based on nothing—just the anticipation. It feels soooo so good and knowing the human brain, it will want more and it will play a trick on you, but that's where the addiction starts. It's the fantasy, the hope, the what-if, and for few seconds, it's the best high you'll ever get. BEFORE YOU EVEN PLACE THE DAMN BET.

Say you're at the casino or at home gambling online. You've got your shrinking stack of chips, you pull the lever/press spin, the reels spin, and BAM! You win. Now this is worse, it's an immediate dopamine hit, it's like your brain got a free shot of adrenaline. The problem is the high doesn't last. You won a few bucks, but what happens next? You're queuing up for another round. It's the dopamine cycle. It's like eating a bag of chips you are saving up for later—you start with one, next thing you're five deep, and by the end, you're like, "What the fuck just happened?" nothing left. Gambling operates the same way, except with higher stakes, you think the next win will make you feel whole, spoiler alert: it won't.

As much as life's unhealthy, fake little dopamine hits are not the solution to your problems, just distractions from the gnawing truth—that most of the shit you're searching for outside yourself? It's all a fucken mirage yes. People who chase endless dopamine hits—whether it's binge watching, playing games, porn or instant gratification—th are essentially looking for a quick fix to avoid dealing with life or those issues at hand. But here's the cold, hard truth. The one you get from gambling isn't real, it's fake, SELF-SABOTAGE. The next time you feel the urge to chase that dopamine high after you just lost—think twice cause you're just adding more zeros to your credit balance while your self-esteem takes a nose dive.

There's a friend of mine who'd often get bored, and the moment he picked up his phone, all he could think about was gambling. He'd dive into online slots, flights and all those gambits even when he knew it was a bad idea. "Just one more game" "If I lose this much I'd stop" he'd say, as if each bet could finally bring him the win he was craving. And you could tell he's enjoying what he's doing and it wasn't fun anymore, it was the chase, the dopamine hit. After a few occurring losses, he'd say "Now is the time, I'll win it back" and go right back in. I'd often ask him, "Why do you always do this every time you are bored ?" He shrugged, no response. The high's short-lived, and all it ever did was keep him stuck in a cycle he couldn't break, it kind of sort became a habit. Spoiler alert: I'm the friend.

Chasing the dopamine rush through gambling is a well-documented behavior that can lead to addiction, often more intensely than other forms of pleasure-seeking behaviors.

The underlying mechanism revolves around how gambling stimulates the brain's reward system. One of the most powerful drivers is the VRRS (variable ratio reinforcement schedule) that gambling follows. Unlike other addictive behaviors that have fixed rewards, gambling offers unpredictable rewards, making it even more addictive because the brain is hardwired to keep chasing that uncertainty. Those who chase this dopamine rush often increase the frequency, duration or amounts as they build tolerance, needing more extreme stimulation to feel the same levels of excitement, Studies estimate that about 1% of the general population suffers from gambling addiction, BUT this number is higher is higher among those who use gambling as a way to "chase" dopamine rush.

Stop chasing fake gambling dopamine hits, and start gambling smart, with a strategy, plan and the knowledge to tilt the odds in your favor. It's all about indulging in the adrenaline rush while maintaining control over impulses and emotions.

What The Fuck Is the Point of This Book?

YOU CAN'T MASTER GAMBLING. This book it isn't some magic airy fairy "cheat-code", life hack or some secret formula that's going to make every bet you place hit, that's all a fugazi. So don't get it twisted, there's no such thing as a guaranteed win, it's about playing smarter, not luckier. And that right there is a real game-changer.

Let's face it—the world of gambling is a freaking minefield. One wrong move, and you could end up knee-deep in financial chaos and emotional wreckage. My chat is, in the world of gambling, THE HOUSE ALWAYS WINS, you can't outsmart it, you can't beat it that's why wise betting matters.

This book is here to guide you through chaos and find success in it, it's your beacon of wisdom in the vast, murky sea of uncertainty. Think of it as your personal GPS to navigate gambling in a way that keeps you safe, sane and (hopefully} ahead of the game. This book will definitely help you understand the psychology behind—and that's half the battle.

In these pages, you'll uncover a treasure trove of strategies, insights, and tips designed to help you make smarter decisions, protect your bankroll, and maybe—just maybe—find a way to enjoy gambling without losing your shirt. Think of it as a guide to responsible play, but it's more than that. It's more like a blueprint for better financial decision-making when it comes to risk and reward. How to approach money with the kind of discipline that can turn you into a savvy player in the tables. You see, the lessons here go beyond gambling. The principles you'll learn—about risk, greed, control, psychology, willpower, and money—are the same ones that apply when making life's decisions. Smart gambling teaches you about delayed gratification, managing impulses, and avoiding emotional decisions that could lead to regret.

Whether you're looking to really understand the odds or just hoping to get your head in the right place before you make your next bet, this book is your guide, a manual guide that shows you how to play smart and responsibly and keeping your head above water in a world that's designed to drown you in temptation.

Remember that responsible gambling is not about avoiding the thrill, but it's about embracing it wisely. In essence, gambling is a delicate between excitement and strategy. By mastering the art of calculated risk-taking, you are not just playing a game, you're orchestrating an epic saga of chance and skill, where now every spin of the wheel, dealt cards and roll of the dice becomes a moment of breathtaking suspense.

This book not only offers valuable insights for gamblers seeking a more calculated and mindful path, but also shares intriguing stories, serving as an invaluable guide to help enrich the reader's understanding.

So yeah, dive into the fray, seize the excitement and let the thrill of the game ignite your senses like never before.

REMEMBER, the house always wins, that's why gambling wisely matters.

INTERLUDE
Personal Reflection

IN THE REALM Of 8th grade memories, year 2018 I enthusiastically embraced the local coin-tossing game known as " zwepe ", with pocket money on the line, friends and I engaged in it, occasionally leading to losses of our pocket money. It seemed harmless at the time, but that was just the start of a long journey into gambling that I didn't realize I was on.

Growing up, my passion and love for football extended beyond just watching games, I was also deeply involved in following player performances, anticipating upcoming matches, and tracking team statistics. Naturally, I engaged in friendly bets with friends and peers—betting on things like who'd score next, or what the final score might be which further fueled my enthusiasm for the sport. At the time this other friend of mine Boitumelo had just purchased the latest gaming Xbox console, oh boy—we'd often make friendly bets or host tourneys with others.

As I progressed to 10th grade, the emergence of online betting opened new avenues for me to engage with football, allowing me to combine my knowledge and passion with strategic wagering on soccer games, fueling a cycle of wins and losses. My pocket money went straight into it week in, week out. It was kind of stressful, but a hobby where I can make money on the side and lose some, but I convinced myself it was "healthy gambling" and I wouldn't see myself in casinos or engage in other gambling methods other than it.

Year 2021, it all came crashing down, culminating in an 800-rand debt to a friend, thanks to betting through online mobile video games, I'd spend every day after school at home, playing the game with the friend, gambling instead of doing my homework. This was during the COVID lockdown, when the world felt like it had slowed down, and the rush of games and gambling was my escape. I was just 16 with an 800-rand debt hanging over me, crazy *innit*. Looking back that's insane. But back then, it just felt like the next thing I had to deal with.

After high school, my foray into intricacies of gambling deepened during my gap year. The allure of mastering various games became irresistible, with every penny I got was dedicated to the pursuit. Well, I had no steady income other than the allowance I got from my rents, so knowing my love for money I had to make more on my own. Gambling seemed to be the only option.

Fast forward that year a job presented an opportunity for increased income, however this siren call of higher stakes and bets, particularly in the South African-most loved game called "Aviator". My betting escalated in ways I can't even define—there was no rational through in it anymore. It was like I was trapped, and even my co-workers could see how hooked I was. Over the course of three months with a job, I lost a significant portion of my earnings equivalent to the cost of an iPhone 11 and still have some left over, vanished into the digital abyss just like that. But I couldn't stop. It just got worse. I started gambling with my transport money, even taking out huge chunks of loans to feed my addiction. I'd spend entire nights—midnight till morning—just depositing and betting, even when I was winning, I was always chasing a bigger win till I lost it. I was stuck in a cycle of deposits and withdrawals, and no matter how much I lost or won, I kept going.

As time went by, I lost money for important things too. I can't go into details, let's just say my parents might be reading this book, and I'd rather not get into all that. But honestly? It's no biggie now.

My addiction took a toll on me. It was a heavy weight I didn't except. I thought I had control. I thought I could stop anytime. But the truth was, gambling had me wrapped up in a way that I wasn't prepared for, and by the time I realized it, I was already too deep. DROWNING is an understatement.

The ensuing struggle with depression prompted a critical self-examination, realizing that the issue was not gambling but rather the recklessness with which I approached it. Revealing the need for a strategic and thoughtful approach. I began to analyze my gambling patterns and habits in detail, identifying various pitfalls that had gone unnoticed and areas where I had consistently fallen short. As I continued to refine and hone my strategies, by following the principles I had uncovered, I was able to transform my approach to gambling, which ultimately resulted in substantial success in my gambling endeavors. This introspection was not only eye-opening but also empowering, as it laid the foundation for " The Complete Gambling Playbook". However, before I could formally create a comprehensive guide, as I continued to refine and hone my strategies, I began collecting a series of valuable tips I came with, insights from people whom I know achieved great things in gambling, and lessons learned through my experiences—how skills like saving my winnings, knowing my limits, and more, would play a crucial role in my transformation. They proved to be vital in many ways, I will dive deeper into these principles in the upcoming chapters, where I will explore each one in greater detail.

Recognizing that others would benefit from the knowledge I had gained, I had the intention of simply sharing my discoveries with a wider audience. However, somehow, the idea of writing the book itself, combining my scrappy collections with stories, stats and more came to me, and I realized that this would be the best way to organize and present everything I had learned. This decision laid the groundwork for the creation of the comprehensive guide—a detailed resource to help others avoid the mistakes and achieve success in their gambling journeys. HOPE IT HELPS.

Start With a Sizeable Bankroll to Give Yourself a Strong Foundation

Before you buy your way into a game, you should have enough to play without second guessing every move you make. One of the most critical factors for success in gambling, be it poker, trading or any other high-stakes endeavor. A strong financial foundation is not just about having enough to play. It's about having the mental space to focus on the game and not constantly worry about your next move or how much you're losing.

The temptation to start with a small bankroll or try to get by with just a little bit of capital is common, especially when you're eager to dive into action or in need to raise money or something. But the truth is when you don't have enough money to absorb losses or make calculated decision, fear starts to take over. Because when your funds are small, every loss or misstep will hurt and you'll begin to make decisions out of fear, lose your sense of control. Having enough will allow you to keep your mind on the game and not on your shrinking stack of chips.

When you're playing with a small bankroll, it's easy to become emotionally attached to every win and loss. You start thinking about your chips not as a tool for making strategic plays but as reflection of your ability to continue playing. This emotional attachment clouds your judgement and creates a vicious cycle: the more fear you feel, the more likely you are to make impulsive decision.

Small bankroll forces you to make short-term decisions driven by the need to preserve the little you have left, rather than long-term strategic plays or risk that could potentially pay off. On the other hand, a healthy start-up provides the security and confidence needed to play your best game. It gives you the breathing room to think strategically and allow you to withstand losses that are certain to happen without feeling the weight of every setback. No matter how skilled you are, every player encounters losing streaks, it's simply part of the process. Losing a few hands or rounds isn't a cause to panic when you know you have the financial cushion to continue playing your game.

A strong bankroll removes the psychological barrier that makes it difficult to stick to your plan. You're no longer constantly worried about losing the money that represents your last hope. Instead, you can focus on optimizing each move. The key is to stick to your strategy and let the statistics play out over time. Patience and discipline are far easier to maintain when your bankroll is strong enough to survive inevitable downswings.

The exact amount depends on the type of gamble you're playing and your risk tolerance. However, the general rule is this: enough money to play multiple rounds without ever feeling the pressure of losing it all.

For example, if you're playing poker, professionals recommend your bankroll should be sufficient to cover anywhere from 20 to 50 buy-ins for the stakes you're playing at. In trading, a simpler rule applies, a friend told me that if you want enough margin volatile fluctuations without the fear of being wiped out on a single bad trade.

This financial buffer is one of the greatest advantages of being a serious player and a winner—one that stays calm under pressure and plays the game to the best of their ability.

Establish Clear Win Goals

Imagine you are in a situation where you're setting yourself up for a financial goal. You've been busting your ass off, and now you are ready to reap the rewards. But here's the thing it's easy to get swept up in the excitement and if you didn't have a specific target in mind, you risk going on an endless pursuit that can lead to nothing but disappointment.

You'll be caught in a never-ending cycle of playing, a gambling session should only last until you've reached either your win goal or lost your max bet, because the probability of losing goes up the longer you play. Greed will push to overstay your welcome, making you think that the next bet will make you richer. Spoiler alert: it won't, the longer you play, the greater the risk of losing what you gained.

Come up with a definite, realistic amount that you hope to win. Define your win goal in clear terms, something tangible that you can measure. Like telling yourself "I want to end the day with at least R3000 "or "I need enough to cover my Spotify and Showmax account for the month" you reach your target, walk away. Don't overthink it or let the moment consume you. Take your winnings and move on, DON'T GET GREEDY.

Greed, indeed is a common human trait, it's human nature. It's something that resides within all of us, particularly surfaces in financial pursuits. When money is on the table, it has a way of captivating our minds. It beckons, it calls, and suddenly we believe there is more to be had. The mind, entangled in illusions often tricks us into thinking that the next win will be just around the corner. We get wrapped up in the idea of more—more profits, more returns. The temptation is to keep playing, inducing the belief that one can achieve greater returns instead of realizing your profits and choosing to cash them out.

November 2023, the UEFA Champions League resumed for its final group-stage matches, attracting significant attention from individuals globally engaged in betting activities.

Abundance of individuals partook in placing bets, sharing bet slips, and engaging in discourse heated discussions regarding match predictions, all amid high favorable odds.

A friend of my friend compiled an ambitious 18 matches bet slip parlay, which yielded an astonishing potential return of R127,000, he only wagered just r20. At first glance, gambling experts would have labelled it as a recipe for failure, that's like setting yourself up for failure. It's a parlay difficult to land.

Day one, everything seemed to be going his way. The first few games went smoothly, and as the day came to a close, the initial success on the first day left for the following day, offering an R8,000 return. Advised to cash it out, greed prevailed, he hesitated. In most situations, this would've been considered a wise choice—guaranteed, solid profit from a modest r20 bet.

What made the situation even more critical was that the parlay itself, with its multiple cash-out opportunities was designed for exactly this kind of scenario—to entice bettors with chance to lock in a profit at various stages

As the second day unfolded, the first half-teams of the parlay played earlier that night and held the lead and the cash out value fluctuated, reaching 13k at its peak. The momentum seemed to be on his side. Friends advised him to take the cash-out, walk away with the R13,000, and avoid the risk of losing it all. Despite counsel to cash out, he grasped to the dream of a massive 127k payout and refused, r127,000—was too powerful to resist, the dream of a life-changing windfall kept him hanging on. If he had set a clear cash-out goal from the start—perhaps aiming to secure the cash-out offered after a certain number of games or value reached at the time, he could've taken the safer option R8,000 or this R13,000, for someone in his situation the amount is significant and 400+ times the wage he put. He continued to chase the full 127k, hoping that few more matches would turn everything in his favor. As the other-half of the games commenced, the bet slip ultimately crumbled with unexpected outcomes, Manchester united, holding a 2-0 lead against Galatasaray, suddenly collapsed in the 2^{nd}half, allowing Galatasaray to come back and win the match.

Cash-out options disappeared. Reality hit hard, he was left devastated, in a state of extreme emotional distress. From an initial investment of 20 bucks the slip transitioned from 8k to 13k at its peak and eventually to zero. He cleverly structured the matches to create massive cash-out opportunities, but there was never a clear win goal, he had multiple chances to secure a profitable outcome—R8,000 on day one, R13,000 on day two—but greed clouded his judgement.

The scholar and unemployed individual missed a chance to alter his circumstances, and instead the story ended in regret.

The bet slip which had once held the promise of R127,000, now amounted to nothing. If he had a clear goal—whether it was after 10/11/12 matches he cashes out or whether it was a profit of r8,000, r10,000 or r13,000—he might've walked away with a life-changing amount for someone his age.

This tale highlights the grip of greed, as the pursuit of an improbable jackpot overshadowed rational decision making.

This cautionary tale underscores the importance of setting win goals and the essential risk of relentless pursuit after a significant payout.

Establishing goals becomes crucial in navigating the allure and potential pitfalls of the gambling world.

Define Your Loss Limits

A loss limit is your ticket to gambling sanity. A loss limit will prevent you from betting more than you can afford. It's the amount you can safely afford to lose on a given day, hand or table—once you've hit that limit, the GAME IS FUCKEN OVER, NO EXCEPTIONS. No "one more bet". The game is done, and you walk away. It's the ultimate way to protect yourself from the emotional whirlwind that gambling can be. It's about drawing a hard line—when you cross it, you're out. Simple, right?

Here's the beauty of it: Your loss limit isn't about winning or losing; it's about controlling how much you stand to lose. You're telling yourself "I can afford to lose X percent of my bankroll today, and I'll only use it to gamble". That percentage/ amount could be anything between 1-25% of your total bankroll. If you stick to this limit, you'll never have to worry about losing it all. Think of it as your financial self-respect—because if you can't respect that, the game will chew you up and spit you out.

Now, think of Archie Karas we mentioned in the previous chapters. If he'd had a solid loss limit in place after few occurring losses, the guy might've been a legend for the right reasons, not saying he's not (he is one of the greatest (and most tragic)) But instead, Archie kept playing until he lost it all because there was no loss limit and if he had one he was going stop at some point and still walk away rich.

Think of the scene from the movie Casino Royale where Daniel Craig, as James Bond, is at the poker table. At one point, he says "I know when to quit". He's got that that air of quiet confidence. That's what a loss limit gives you; the ability to know when exactly to quit. Bond's cool, calculated demeanor isn't just for action scenes—it's a metaphor for knowing your limits in life. You don't need to be Bond to make smart financial decisions. You just need to know when the game's over and walk away with your dignity intact.

So, my advice? Set your loss limit. Could be 5%, 15% or even 1%—whatever helps you sleep at night. But here's the key: STICK TO IT. And if you ever get tempted to push beyond it, just remember Archie Karas and how quicky it all vanished.

Name your loss limit, as long as you stick to your loss limit, you'll never have to worry about going broke.

Gambling Finances: Separate Accounts & Gambling Budget

Gambling—whether it's a roulette wheel, poker, sports betting or even online games—has its own set of rules. But beyond knowing the game rules, there's one golden rule that you must follow if you want to succeed as a gambler: Managing your money like a pro. Trust me, without control over your bankroll, you might as well be tossing coins in the air and hoping they land in your favor.

The most successful gamblers didn't get there by risking everything in their bank accounts. They built systems and boundaries.

First thing's first: SEPARATE YOUR GAMBLING FROM YOUR PERSONAL FINANCES. It's the equivalent of keeping your work life and your personal life separate. You wouldn't be taking personal calls in a sale call with a client or your boss (unless you're secretly living on the edge). So don't mix your personal savings with gambling funds.

The ability to control, preserve and build the money you start out with is essential for finding success as a gambler. So, you can even open a separate account. With a dedicated account, you'll be able to play without worrying about dipping into your savings and personal accounts. You will play with a purpose, set a specific amount aside just for gambling, and that's all you can use. Your savings? Off-limits, your rent money? Definitely off-limits. This will allow you to keep your gambling pursuits and your everyday life separate.

NEVER take money out of your personal savings to finance your gambling stakes and habits. That's a slippery slope.

I myself at first thought I could handle the thrill of gambling without any real boundaries. It all started with a few hundred bucks from the money meant for other things and then gradually began taking a little more from the account every time I lost. This led to taking loans. long story short,

I got deep into the red, and my debt piled up faster than I could win. By the time io realized it was a mess. Mind you this happened multiple times, if I had just opened a separate gambling account, I could've kept my financial life in check and enjoyed gambling without the constant stress.

Now that you've separated your funds, let's talk BUDGETING. It's tempting to keep throwing money into the game when you've won. After all, the wins just keep rolling in, right? Well, not exactly. The key here is discipline. A gambling budget is like a diet plan for your finances. Set aside a specific amount from your winnings, the way you would for your groceries and other expenses. Save some of your winnings or put them towards your necessities and spend some of it on yourself.

Never attempt to try to return your winnings. Returning your winnings, gambling again trying to win more especially after a significant win, can be tempting, but it's decision that can have long-term consequences for your gambling success. The trap here is called recency bias, you've just had a big win, so you think you can outsmart the game and win more with your winnings, so your brain starts thinking you're invincible. Doing so not only creates a dangerous psychological pattern whereby winning becomes associated with giving back but also undermines your confidence and discipline. Moreover, this negative reinforcement perpetuates the idea that losing is acceptable while eroding the profitability and potential of your wins. By returning your winning you miss out on opportunities to reinvest in future bets or build your bankroll

Therefore, it's crucial to resist the urge to return winning. Celebrate your wins responsibly and use them wisely to enhance your long-term success in gambling.

Bankroll management like separating accounts and budgeting is one of the top reasons professional gamblers win in the long run. In fact, a study by Gambling With Lives, which analyzed successful gambling strategies, found that those who separated their gambling funds and saved their winning or spent them wisely had a 50% higher chance of staying profitable over time.

Quit While You're Ahead

When you're winning: Here's the golden nugget that most gamblers are too dumb to realize: The real key to gambling success is recognizing when it's time to quit. And I mean really quit and go, not some half-hearted "I'll play just one more hand and then I'm out" nonsense, because let's face it, where all know where that leads. You've probably heard that saying a thousand times: "Real gamblers know when to quit". Yeah, it sounds like some corny bullshit you'd read in a self-help book or on a motivational meme, but it's actually true.

So, after winning big, two or three times you can be sure your fortunes are about to shift, that's when you should cash in your moola and call it a day. Remember, the longer you keep playing, the more the odds begin to favor the house. This isn't just some vague philosophical idea—it's a cold, hard mathematical reality and I'm not talking about some abstract concept, I'm talking about actual numbers. Gambling casinos and games are not in the business of making you rich—they're in the business of making themselves rich, and guess what? They're really good at it.

Now let me school you, let's say you bet r5 on a spin and you play 50 spins in a row. The machine has a 5% house edge (a typical rate for many slot machines). Every spin, you're statistically giving the house a portion of your bet. You might hit a lucky streak and win a couple, but over the course of 50 spins, you're likely to lose R12,50 on average by the time you're done. Remember, that's just the **average** loss. So, no matter how many "lucky streaks" you hit, in the long run if you keep playing for hours you will lose it all, you're fighting against a much stronger opponent than you. That's because, over time, the house edge does its work—slowly, methodically and ruthlessly. It's just the way the game is designed.

When you're losing: Now let's talk about when things start to go sideways. Losing sucks, it's like getting slapped in the face by Mark Henry. The problem is it's emotional, losing is not just about the money; it's also about your ego, pride, and your irrational belief that you can outwit fate with the sheer force of will. It's the exact same thing that happens when you get dumped and immediately text back saying "we should totally be together, I will change" Spoiler alert: you haven't changed. And neither has the game.

Resist the temptations to CHASE YOUR LOSSES, Otherwise, you're only setting yourself up to lose even more, trust me I've been there. It's like trying to get out of debt by taking out another credit card. It's a cycle of despair, and you're just digging yourself a much deeper hole you are already in. If you're in a losing streak, the truth is you're not going to turn it around. I've been that idiot, it gets to a point whereby you're no longer losing your money, but your fucking mind. That's when the emotional floodgate open, you start playing with your feelings, not your head and that's a slippery slope.

Chasing losses can quickly turn into a full-blown addiction. Every loss starts feeling like a personal attack, you start investing more and more cash, even the wins that follows, instead of feeling good, you feel relief. Relief that the nightmare might be over. That's the moment you know you've fucked up. Every time I'd lose, I'd try to buy my way back in, thinking I could make up for what I lost. I'd keep doubling down, pulling out more money like a dumbass, *fuuuuuuuck dude (*in Chris Williamson's voice*).* It was an emotional spiral, like trying to fill a bottomless pit with a garden hose. You never get ahead, it's a futile exercise.

If you find yourself stuck in this cycle, it's a sign you might be on the edge of addiction or already there. And I'm not talking about casual gambling problem. I'm talking about that feeling when you're so emotionally invested that you can't think straight anymore. You start justifying your losses to yourself "If I just keep going, I'll make it all back, It's just a temporary setback". That's when you know you've crossed the line.

If you're losing and probably lost your max bet or limit, walk away. The hardest part is stopping. It's like trying to quit smoking or stop eating that junk food. But you've got to do it. Don't try to fix what can't be fixed. Walk the fuck away, because chasing those losses isn't going to get you anything except more stress, more desperation, and a whole lot of regret. Definitely not worth it.

If you're losing, quit.

Handling The Risk Paradox

Be willing to take risks, while playing it safe is usually the wisest course but sometimes you have to take a LEAP OF FAITH in order to come out on top. Playing it safe is usually your best bet, it's comfortable, it's much more predictable, and in most cases it's what keeps the bills paid and the lights on. On the other hand, there are moments in life—sometimes fleeting, sometime painfully obvious—when you have to take huge risks. It's those moments when you're on the field, the ball is at your feet, and you have to decide: take the shot at goal or pass it to a teammate for a better opportunity.

Here's the paradox: While it's generally a good idea to avoid risks, sometimes risk is the only thing that can get you ahead, that shot at goal could've made you the top scorer in your league. But here's the kicker—before you make reckless decisions, you need to take a deep breath, assess the situation and if you've weighed all the possible outcomes carefully, there's a good chance that your confidence will be rewarded. It's all about risk management.

The best time to take risks is when you are down a little but stand to win a lot. Say you're at a slot machine, and you've already burned through a few spins with no luck, you're not out of chips yet but you're not exactly hitting the jackpot either but you've kind of analyzed the pattern. So, what do you do? Do you keep playing it safe, hoping for a small win? The thing is those small wins will come in cycles. You'll hit a few, feel like you're on the up, then watch as the machine takes back what you've earned in the next few spins. It's now a back—and—forth, a push—and—pull—win, lose, win, lose. Yeah, sure good for you, the key is to stay in the game long enough, knowing that the tide can turn anytime. But sometimes a bold move is what will reward you, it might seem risky, but when it lands, it can leave you with a win bigger than you expected, then now you leave the game pockets full. It's about reading the situation, knowing when to take the chance, and understanding that sometimes you need to bet big to get big. It's about making calculated moves where the reward outweighs the potential loss.

It's how it works, even in real-life situations. Take Steve Jobs, for example. He didn't just wake up one day and say "Hey I'm starting a comp-company" and boom—Apple was born. No, Steve was willing to take risks, but he also knew when to step back. Apple's early days were far from glamorous. Steve Job's was booted from the company he founded, and yet he kept swinging—went back to the drawing board, made calculated risks, and eventually turned things around. By the time the iPhone launched, he had already weighed the risks of failure and seen the potential rewards. He took the leap of faith only when it mattered, and he did it with wisdom, not desperation.

NEVER rush into a losing situation out of desperation. This is where things get little tricky. There's a fine line between calculated risk and reckless desperation. It's like that one friend who always wants to invest in "the next big thing" even though their track record is full of bad decisions. "Broskie, I swear this time it's gonna work out" Yeah, sure. Desperate moves tend to lead to more desperation. If you're already down, but you're not completely out, the worst thing you can do is jump into a risky situation just because you're desperate for a win. It's like putting your last R100 and betting it all on a single aviator flight game. Yeah, the high is so intoxicating, but the low? OUCH. The point is, don't risk your future on a gamble just because you're feeling a little "off" right now, most times in gambling and finance the best risk is waiting for a better moment.

The key to handling the risk paradox is finding that sweet spot where your confidence and caution. You want to be brave enough to take calculated risks, but not so eager to prove yourself that you leap without a plan. You want to be wise enough to understand that not all risks are worth taking. In the end, it's not about always taking the safest route, nor is it about being a reckless cowboy. It's about understanding the landscape of risk and reward and making the decisions you can live with—win or lose. Because life doesn't come with a manual, but it sure comes with lot of risks. Handle them wisely, and you might just find yourself on the winning side of the paradox. In the book Rich Dad, Poor Dad (just finished reading it a month ago), Robert Kiyosaki talks about how playing it safe and avoiding risks can actually be more dangerous than taking calculated risks. He emphasizes that people who play it too safe by sticking to the status quo often miss out on opportunities for growth and financial freedom. I remember he said something along the lines of "The main reason people play it safe is fear, they fear losing money or making mistakes, but in reality, it's the fear of not taking risks that can cause greater harm in the long run." The underlying message is that avoiding risks may seem like a safe strategy, but it can lead to missed opportunities for wealth-building. Instead, Kiyosaki encourages people to embrace risk, and take smart financial risks. This also goes for trading and investing.

But remember, desperation is a bad wingman. Keep your head cool, and you'll find that risk isn't always the enemy, it's your fucken fear.

Staying Focused

Whilst playing, imagine that nothing in the world exists. Stressing out about school, work or going over your plans for the weekend that will require money could end up costing you. If you allow yourself to get distracted by these thoughts, the cost can be significant—both financially and mentally. The key to gambling success (yeah, I know there are too many keys, might as well have a key holder *innit mate*) lies in your ability to stay focused, blocking out everything that isn't directly related to the game at hand. It's not just about playing; it's about being fully present, making each decision with clarity and purpose. When you are gambling, it's essential to eliminate as many outside distractions as possible, try to tune out the commotion going on around you. This might mean finding a quiet space or turning off notifications on your phone. You need to create some sort of mental space where only the game matters. Your mind must be clear and ready to engage fully with what's in front of you.

Take, for instance, a person who is gambling while thinking about a work deadline that's fast approaching and requires the immediate attention. This person might start making hasty decisions or act impulsively due to stress, which is detrimental to both the game and their well-being. Gambling, in this case, is no longer a controlled, strategic activity but a way to escape from the looming pressures of life or you are *prolly* addicted. However, instead of finding relief, they end up making poor decisions, losing more money, and increasing their stress. This is an example of how external distractions can cloud judgement and impair your ability to play effectively.

Imagine another scenario where someone is gambling in a taxi while on the way to work (oh man—I used to do that every single fucken time, especially after payday). The noise of the car and of the people inside the taxi, the rush of traffic, the multiple stops—all these external factors will prevent the person from fully focus.

It's important to understand that gambling is not a task to be done mindlessly. It's a mental game that requires careful thought, strategic planning, and concentration.

One key technique for maintaining focus is to take breaks frequently, while it may seem counterintuitive to step away from the action, short breaks can actually help you come back with a refreshed perspective and a clearer mind. This will not only allow you to regain your energy, but it also helps you avoid pitfalls of overextending yourself mentally. Gambling requires focus, and trying to power through a long stretch of gameplay without a break can lead to fatigue and mental fog, not only that but remember the longer you play, the more the odds begin to favor the house and you will lose, because the slot machine for example won't hit jackpot every spin.

Think of it like running a marathon. You wouldn't expect to run 26 miles without pacing yourself or taking a drink of water, right? In the same way, you need to pace yourself when gambling. Also, staying focused isn't just about blocking distractions; it's about setting clear intentions for each session. Before you even start gambling, define what you want to achieve as I've explained about win goals. Are you playing for fun, or do you have a specific financial goal in mind? Knowing why you're playing will help you focus and make better decisions along the way. It also helps you remind yourself of your limits or time frame for your session. These parameters are essential.

Staying focused also requires managing your emotions. Imagine you're on a losing streak. Frustration begins to build.

The more you lose, the more you feel like you need to win back what you've lost. This emotional reaction is what often leads to chasing losses, a dangerous mindset that can quickly spiral out of control. A focused gambler, on the other hand, will recognize the emotional trigger, acknowledge it, and step back before making a rash decision that might worsen the situation. By staying calm and rational, the focused gambler maintains control over their game and their emotions, leading to better decisions in the long run.

In conclusion, staying focused in everything that involves financial risks is one of the most crucial skills for success. It involves blocking out distractions, managing your emotions, setting clear intentions, and pacing yourself with regular breaks. So, the next time you gamble, remember: the world around you can wait.

Losses Are Inevitable

Every gambler dreams of that moment—when the cards fall perfectly into place, when luck seems to favor them, and they walk away with a big payout that changes everything. It's easy to get fixate on the idea that if you play, you'll eventually get the payout you deserve. But the reality is that losses are inevitable. It's like the weather—no matter how many times you check the weather forecast or plan for sunny skies, there's always a chance of rain. Some days, the storm comes early. You didn't plan it, you didn't see it coming, but it's there, and it's going to drench you. That's how losses work. And as much as you wish you could avoid them, they're bound to happen. The same way nobody can escape a busy, bad day at work, or a relationship that falls apart, or a dream that slips out of your grasp. It's all part of a game.

The problem is, we hate losing. We hate the sting, the humiliation, the anger that follows. It's easy to spiral into that negative space where every loss feels like the end of the world. Sometimes things just won't go your way. The sooner you accept that fact, the better. Because the more you resist losses, the more they'll crush your confidence. Imagine trying to play cards but freaking out every time you lose a hand—eventually, you're too afraid to make any real moves. You're frozen, and that's the trap most of us fall into—we're so terrified of losing that we stop playing altogether, and that's how you'll miss the opportunity to win.

Now, I'm not saying you should enjoy losses. No one likes to lose. But if you can start seeing them as they are—not setbacks but opportunities to learn, you'll be in a much stronger position. Think of every loss like a free lesson, a harsh one, sure but a lesson nonetheless.

For example, me and the boys realized there are just certain teams we never put on our parlay, but bet them in a different strategy. Now we learned what to do and how to actually approach those situations with more caution and more confidence. And the losses will come, it will happen, probably sooner than you think—embrace it as part of the process. Take a step back, analyze what went wrong, and then get back in the game. You might lose again, and that's okay, it's gambling after all. The trick is to lose in ways that teaches you how to win the next time around, and that's the real payoff. This goes for trading, whether it's stocks, bonds or day-to-day trades.

So, my chat is, in gambling losses are bound to happen and you should get used to that, you are more likely to lose than win. Matter of fact, you should go to the game knowing that you might not come back with your money. The problem is when you become entitled, thinking you deserve to win and you have money problems that needs a big win.

CHAPTER 3: REFINING YOUR STYLE OF PLAY

Narrow Down Your Specialty

When it comes to gambling, the temptation to dive into every game and every sport is real. It's like walking into a casino, and instead of just picking one game to play, you decide to try your hand at roulette, poker, slots, and even that game that looks like a slot machine with a weird wheel (I think it's money wheel or whatever). There is also sports bets, like football, basketball, tennis, horse racing, esports—you name it. Thye are all tempting to try, right? But here's the truth, you can't be good at everything, you can't predict basketball matches if you are not watching it the same way you watch football. You can't be good at flight games if you don't know their rhythms and time frames.

Each of these games has it's own set of rules, strategies and nuances. Some are complex, like poker and cards, where understanding the psychology of your opponent can be just as important as the cards in your hand. Others like roulette, are all about luck and MATH (but mostly luck, let's be honest). I have a friend who's very good at math, so, this one time, there we were, all glued to our phones like zombies. And then out of nowhere, my friend Omphile—the math genius decides to ditch the digital distractions. He grabs a book and a pen, and start scribbling down calculations like a mad scientist. Yeah, sure, okay. But here's the kicker: a few minutes later, he picks up his phone, opens the Hollywood bet app then goes to the roulette section, and bam—consecutive wins. Not just a lucky round, but consecutive wins. Like a freaking cheat code was unlocked. We were all left sitting there, like someone just invented fire in front of us. What blew our minds wasn't just the wins, it was the math he applied—the calculated logic that turned a stupid live roulette game into a predictable outcome. And here's the thing, while we were mindlessly scrolling, he was busy figuring out how to hack life. That moment was a slap in the face. My chat is he applied his math knowledge into a game that required math and because he's so good at math, he thrived but the same math he applied won't work in other games, So, in conclusion, his specialty is roulettes.

Get to the point where you can walk into a card game, sit down, and immediately start sizing up your opponents like you're some sort of betting Sherlock Holmes. Or maybe you want to master the art of sports betting, where you're able to break down the stats, analyze trends and patterns, and be able to love the sport and watch it frequently. In investing, you might want to own a little bit of stocks in Apple, Tesla, Glencore, and maybe a couple of bonds, properties. But do you really think Warren Buffet has a portfolio that includes 15 different kinds of real estate, bonds, stocks, and maybe some cryptocurrencies for fun? No, I doubt that, he sticks to what he knows. His specialty is value investing, and he's damn good at it, like my friend is with live roulettes and my aunt is with playing cards.

Sports betting requires an understanding of stats, trends, and form. You'll have to study team dynamics, injury reports, weather conditions, and a bunch of other factors to make the most informed bets. If you love analyzing stats and playing detective, this could be your sweet and safe spot. Alternatively, maybe you're a strategist at heart. Type of person who enjoys several moves ahead, in that case poker could be your calling, remember it's about reading people, understanding psychology, and knowing when to bluff. Roulette and slots? Well, let's be honest. It's the "wild children" of the casino world—fun, fast and easy to play. You basically rely on luck here. And don't even get me started on Lotto's, the odds of making a fortune are about as good as finding a needle in a haystack for 5minutes.

The point here is to avoid becoming a jack-of-all-trades, master of none. Mastery requires time, practice and patience. You won't get there by hopping from one game to another. Think of building it as building a foundation, once you've got your specialty down, you can branch out and experiment with other areas, but it all starts with one thing. So, pick your game, one or two outlets and devote yourself to learning everything you can about it. The rest will follow, and who knows? Maybe one day you'll be the person other gamblers turn to for advice. Just the way my friends, acquaintances (even girls) come to me for sports parlays.

There are 100s of different games and sports to bet on, each with its unique set of rules and style of play.

Analyze Patterns and Odds

One of the most critical skills a gambler can develop is the ability to analyze patterns and odds. Gambling is not just about blind luck; successful gamblers constantly evaluate the probabilities, trends, and underlying mechanics of games, adjusting their strategies accordingly. By doing so, they transform what might seem like a game of chance into a contest of skill and informed decision-making. So, amigo let's explore how analyzing patterns and understanding odds can significantly improve your gambling approach.

Odds are the foundation of gambling decisions. Odds represent the probability of a particular event occurring, and they serve as a baseline for most gambling decisions. They are typically expressed in three forms: Fractional odds (e.g 5/1), these show how much you stand to win relative to your stake, for every R1 you wager, you'll win R5 IF the event occurs. Decimal odds (e.g 6.00), these show the total payout (stake + profit) you'd receive for every R1 bet, for example, betting R10 at 6.00 odds results in a R60 payout—R50 profit and R10 stake. Money line odds (e.g +500 or -300), you're probably not familiar with these as many online gambling games in our region (South Africa) they're rarely used. Each type of odds translates into probabilities. For example, fractional odds of 5/1 imply a 1 in 6 chance (or approximately 16.67%) of the event happening (yeah, yeah I used a calculator, don't judge, im not really good at math). By understanding these numbers, you can start assessing whether a bet is worth the risk or if the odds are stacked against you.

Patterns are the hidden signals, in many gambling games, outcomes often appear random but may contain subtle patterns that experienced players can identify. Like the way these patterns can be seen in games like aviator and slots to poker hands, and recognizing them can enhance your strategic decisions. Analyzing these patterns can provide you with an edge over other players who might be relying on luck alone. In flight games like aviator, there seems to be a recurring pattern where certain numbers or odds appear repeatedly, giving you a sense of what's likely to happen next. For example, if you notice four consecutive "blues" (or whatever the indicator might be), there's a strong chance that the 5th flight will actually take off and reward you. It could even keep rewarding you for two or three more flights, or do a two "blue"—one "pink"—two "blue"—one "pink" pattern. However, after that, it's as if the system knows it's time to change things up, and you'll see a sudden drop in flights. At that point, everything feels like it's just waiting to "fall"—and it's gonna fall on you like a bad joke at a stand-up-show: unexpected, but somehow inevitable. When betting on sports, patterns manifest in the form of team perfomance, individual player stats, and even historical head-to-head matchups. For example, if a football team has been consistently winning at home and performing poorly away, that is a pattern you can leverage when placing bets. Similarly, analyzing past seasons' statisticss can highlight trends in player performance—some players are on their peak form against other teams (like Mohammed Salah is against Manchester United), so chances are if you bet on him to score, its more likely to happen. The more you analyze such trends, the better you can predict how a game might unfold. For instance, if a team is consisitently outperforming other teams and scoring more during the 2nd half, you may choose to wager in alignment with that pattern.

Undetrstanding and analyzing both odds and patterns is critical because it allows you to make informed-decisions, minimize the element of luck and increasing your chances of success. By continously evaluating the odds, you can better manage your bankroll and avoid placing bets with unfavorable probabilities. Similarly, by recognizing patterns, you can adjust your strategy to exploit opportunities that less observant players might miss.

But this is gambling, so everything has it's pitfalls. So, it's essential to remain cautious about over-interpreting patterns that may not actually exist. You can go wrong, this is a common pitfall known as what psychologist refers to as "pattern bias, where gamblers see pattern in random data. For example, a simple sequence of 1 blue flight followed by 4 pink flights and so on, doesn't indicate a hot streak, but we gamblers sometimes fall into the trap of assuming it does. Because slots and those flight games operate on a random number generators, this is simply an illusion, and the odds of winning on another flight thinking it's due for another 4 consecutive pink flights are just as random as hititng the blue one. Recognizing the difference between true patterns and coincidences is a skill that takes time to develop, but it's a vital for long-term success.

Analyzing patterns and odds is not just about memorizing statistics or being able to count cards—it's about developing a deeper understanding of how gambling works. As you refine your style of play, remember that gambling is a game of probabilities, not certainties. While patterns and odds can give you an edge, always be aware of the risks and be prepared o adjust your strategy based on evolving circumstances. The more you practice analyzing these elements, the sharper your decision-making will become, ultimately improving your gambling outcomes.

Records of Your Wins and Losses

If you're gambling and not keeping track of your wins and losses, are you really gambling smart? It's like going to the gym and not counting reps—sure, you're moving your body but are you really getting stronger? Yeah, I know it's a bad example to use, I suck at those I know. Keeping a record of your gambling wins and losses is essential for more than just tracking your financials. It's about understanding the entire psychology of your bets and your instincts. The act of recording forces you to confront reality. For example, Dating, you might convince yourself you're a catch, but if you never analyze your dating history, you're doomed to keep picking the same not so 10s and toxic partners. Similarly, if you don't review your losses and wins, you'll just keep making the same dumb betting decisions and not knowing if whether gambling works for you. Kemoikantse, a friend of mine who has a total deposit of R24,000 and a total withdrawal of R5,800, he's currently playing the losing game and every time he win he gets happy, but the truth is he's been donating and his goal is to go broke for the thrill of it, that's not a winning strategy. If he had kept a record of his deposits(bets) and wins(withdrawal) he could've slowed down or quit early, but it was later this year when we were checking our statements of transactions.

This isn't some high-maintenance spreadsheet you need to fill out every 30 seconds (unless that's your thing—then go for it). Every time you deposit or maybe you at the casino, write the amount you went in with, the same thing applicable when you win(withdraw) to see if whether you are making a profit or not. it's not even about the numbers (money). There are some records you can track that can help. Start simple: DATE AND TIME, It's basic, but you'll notice patterns if you look closely.

Are you more prone to losing late night? Or each time you bet on Tuesday night UEFA games than your regular Saturday league games. GAME TYPES: Which one brings more moola most of the time. You might realize you're donating more on parlays than the slots that always has you on edge and chow your R100 in 3minutes thinking. Tracking your wins and losses is like installing a GPS in your car. You need to know where you are to figure out how to get to where you want to go. Sure, you might get lucky and stumble into success without a map, but more often than not, you'll end up circling the same block, wondering why you are stuck in the same spot or even worse you are heading into a different wrong direction.

Let's face it: everyone has their "hot streaks" and "cold streaks". It's part of the gambling world. But if you don't keep a record of these, you're just chasing random highs and lows without any real strategy. Worse, you may think your luck is "turning around" when, in reality, you're just on a tail end of a losing streak, like this other friend of mine, Refentse. He only won once and that was it, he doesn't realize that all he does is to keep donating to the thrill. And every time he makes loans to bet on his-ambition made parlays with a +R1000 debt hanging around him already, he doesn't realize he's been making dumb bets for the last 6 months.

The power of trends: It might feel like you're just writing down a bunch of meaningless numbers. But after a while, you'll start seeing patterns. For instance, you might notice you always win when you play aviator for just 20 minutes but lose when you play for an hour or more. That's a trend worth knowing. Once you start identifying such trends, you can start tailoring your gambling habits to maximize the good days and minimize the bad ones.

So, if you're serious about improving your game, get comfortable with keeping records. And by comfortable, I mean don't let it feel like homework. It's just part of the process, a necessary one. And the more you do it, the more you'll see how useful it really is. This will allow you to track your progress over time and manage your bankroll effectively, profits and losses. You'll be your own fucken accountant bruh.

Master Your Emotions: The Psychological Edge

Let's be real—emotions aren't these lovely, cuddly, doodled-up thingies you see in greeting/invitation cards. They're messy, unpredictable, and sometimes downright painful, they don't always make sense. They hit you when you least expect it, leaving you raw and exposed, questioning everything. But that's what makes them real, I guess.

You can have all the perfect strategies and know the odds better than the gambling games or casino's own algorithm, but if you can't keep your cool, if you can't manage the emotional rollercoaster that comes with every bet, then you're as good as the guy who bets his whole paycheck on a coinflip just to feel something. Emotions are very powerful—and in gambling, they are a double-edged sword. You can go wrong about it, mastering them isn't just important but essential. Emotional control isn't just a nice-to-have—it's the difference between having a good night at the office (gambling world) and going home broke.

Let's talk about what really happens in your brain when you are in motion gambling. Yes, the stakes are high, tension is thick, the adrenaline? Skyrocket, that's what keeps you coming back for more. Your body releases dopamine when you win as we've explained in the dopamine chapter, that addictive chemical that tricks you into believing you're in control. When you lose, cortisol surges through your system—stress, anxiety, regret. It's a push-pull that tugs at your gut every time you place the bet. But now the problem is, if you let these chemicals dictate your actions, you're not playing the game my friend—you're being played. Say you've just hit a streak of bad luck. Your chips are dwindling, and you can feel your heart rate rising. That rush of frustration or desperation you feel? That's your emotional self, trying to hijack the rational part of your brain. Your decisions now become less about strategy and more about proving something to yourself, to the game, to the world. It's never really about your pocket anymore. You chase losses, the last amount you put you just want to win it back and that one before it. You double down in hopes that the tides will turn. And before you know it, you're in deep shit, a whole fucken hole, saying like the one in apocalypto where the dude hid his family it's an understatement. You've probably experienced the *Tilt* if you're a gambler. That moment when you're take the wheel and the rational side of your brain is locked in the trunk, screaming to get out. I've seen my friend betting on tennis games at 00:00, he doesn't even watch it, doesn't know the players nor the rules and all its bs. It was after his well-safe-made football parlays failed to hit, and he had already made plans with the winnings before he even won. When you win, you get that rush—excitement. It feels great, and it makes you wanna go again and chase it, but it also clouds your judgement making you think you "The man" you are in control, you got this. That little voice "you've got this, one more bet" Is your emotions talking, not your rational brain. You might think you're thinking clearly in the moment, but you're not. Emotions cloud your judgement like a fog rolling over a highway. It's like driving blindfolded. Sure, you might make it through the fog, but most likely, you'll crash.

Here's the truth—Gambling it's about playing the long game, every decision you make should be based on calculated thinking, not on a wild emotional wild reaction. The key to consistently winning isn't to the jackpot every time, it's to make better decisions over time, regardless of what the outcome is in short term. Emotional control gives you what the psychologist refer to as the *psychological edge*, when you can play without your emotions running the show, you are immune to the most dangerous aspect of gambling: e.g the compulsive need to make up for losses. Let me break it down to you why managing your emotions is essential and how you can manage them.

Emotions are a form of bias, a walking, talking bag of cognitive biases. And when you throw gambling into the mix, those biases only get worse. When you're emotional, your brain starts looking for patterns that aren't there. You might convince yourself that you're on the verge of a winning streak after a couple of wins, or you might be certain that the next round is "due" for a win after a series of losses. This is your brain working against you—looking for patterns in randomness, trying to force order on chaos. So, keep your emotions in check at all times, you can recognize these biases for what they are and making decisions based on logic instead of emotional reasoning. There's a thing called "The Equanimo of Gambling" (Yeah, I came up with this shitty phrase baby), it might sound like a joke to you, but there is something to the idea of "equanimo" in gambling (Equanimo it's just a term derived from the word "equanimity" which means mental calmness, stability and composure, esp in difficult situations, it suggests a sense of inner balance and emotional control). To get to this level, you need to see every win and every loss as just part of the process. It's not really personal, yeah, yeah, I get it's about money so I's kind-of is personal, but really? It's not (oh—and remember in chapter 1 I said you should only gamble with money you can afford to lose). Know that you're just a participant in a game of chance, doing your best to make out of it, you win it's not like you're a genius or some, you lose it's not like you're a failure. I'm not trying to sound like a motivational speaker or some. Adopt this "equanimo" mindset, you'll notice few things happen. Your decision-making improves because you're not attached to any outcome, you stop sabotaging yourself by trying to force wins even when you can tell it's a bad day. You find that you're much more resilient in the face of adversity, a string of losses won't break you, it's just another bad day. You won't beat yourself up because you'll know, deep down, that the next opportunity is just around the corner.

Loss-chasing is like chasing a high you can never quite reach, it happens after you lost your money or few bets and you start feeling that gnawing need to win it all back. Doing so leads to bigger losses as you know, not recovery. So, the only way to avoid this trap is by managing your emotions and accepting that loss is just part of the game. And only you can control how you react to it, it's some willpower and grit typa shit that's going to work for you, man up and just don't chase them. You can manage these emotions like a pro, it's not some "you just need to meditate" nonsense, it's a practical advice. Know your limits as we've explained the importance of it and stick to them, it's hard to not break them but when you feel the need to break those limits just know that you're on a tilt and recognize it so you can take a deep breather and take a break from everything. Practice emotional awareness (There are several books, audiobooks and podcasts on that), if you notice yourself getting frustrated, anxious, or overly excited, it might be the best time to take a step back. It's easy to ignore these emotions whilst you're playing, but recognizing them is the first step to managing them. The best gamblers learn to detach from their feelings and take a step back. They don't get greedy when things go well, and they surely don't get desperate when things go poorly.

Mastering your emotions isn't just about being a stoic monk in the face of a losing streak. Itr's about recognizing that your emotions are powerful, but not letting them hijack your decision-making process. The psychological edge you gain by mastering your emotions will carry you further than any strategy ever could. And that's the real key to not just surviving—but thriving—in this world of uncertainty and risk. Every time you gamble, ask yourself this: are you in control or is your emotional state in control of you? Because that difference my friend, will determine whether you're playing for the long haul—or just another victim of the game. Emotional control isn't something that comes naturally to everyone, but it's something you can work on.

CHAPTER 4: THE SLIPPERY SLOPE FALLACY; ADDICTION AWARENESS

Preoccupation With Gambling

Gambling begins as a simple form of entertainment. For many, it's just a way to enjoy night out, test their luck to make extra money, or experience the excitement of a betting game, but mostly it's really to make money on the side. However, for others it becomes much more than a passing pastime. It transforms into an obsession—a preoccupation that takes over their day-to-day thoughts, behavior and life. Preoccupation with gambling is more than just thinking about it occasionally, it's when gambling starts to dominate your thoughts, impacting your emotional state and daily functioning. It becomes the thing you're most focused on, the thing you can't stop thinking about, even when you're not actively gambling. This preoccupation often leads to a pattern whereby an individual thinks about gambling even when they are engaged in other activities, they now start to plan their day around opportunities to gamble, feels anxious or restless when unable to gamble and relies on gambling as a means to escape from stress or any other form of negative emotions. It's this constant mental engagement with gambling that signals the shift from casual involvement to a serious problem. This is a total mindfuck. Once gambling becomes a central focus of your thoughts and actions, it's no longer about fun or recreation—it's about compulsion.

It's a major red flag when gambling starts to interfere with your work, school or daily life. Like when you start gambling during working hours or when you're busy, this behavior can quickly spiral, missing deadlines, making mistakes due to distractions, you can't even socialize with people. Intentionally doing only half of your tasks so you can go back to gambling, even to the extent of procrastinating work that must be done, it can be chores or running errands and when it starts to take up more and more of your time, spending entire days at the casino or gambling late into the night, neglecting other responsibilities. You wake up? Gamble, you are taking a poo, dump or whatever? Gamble, just got in a taxi? Gamble, this is a slippery slope and it's all in your subconscious. When other activities like your hobbies no longer seem interesting or satisfying, they all take a backseat when gambling takes over. I remember there was a time I was consumed by online betting and started to cancel plans more frequently, postponing my daily routines like gym and reading. The things that once brought joy seemed trivial compared to the obsession I had developed with betting. You even feel anxious or restless when unable to gamble

Preoccupation with gambling doesn't happen in a vacuum—it's driven by a complex cycle of emotions and psychological triggers we've covered in previous chapters. One I didn't mention it's what we call the near miss effect, this phenomenon occurs when a person feels like they were just one step away from winning—such as hitting almost the right combination of cards or numbers, these "near misses" encourage gamblers to keep playing, so they never stop playing regardless of the situation or commotion they are in, because they believe their win is just around the corner. It's almost similar to the hope of recouping losses or the thrill of winning.

· · During my tenure at Man Trucks and Bus at Centurion, I was working as a parts picker and it was a big workshop so I'd often hide in the shelves and take out my phone and gamble whilst I was sent to pick or pack certain parts, I'd take time because I was gambling, I just couldn't stop. It was as if I was stuck in a dilemma if whether I was gambler who goes to work or a worker who likes to gamble. Even on my way to work or back from work I'd gamble the whole way ignoring friends and colleagues in the transport. I was always moody as fuck, my day was always determined by how I did in the slots/flights/roulettes.

When gambling becomes the center of someone's world, the ripple effect on their life can be significant. Being always preoccupied with gambling affects not only you it but also your relationships, work life and overall mental health. The more time you spent engaging in gambling, the less time is available for family, friends and meaningful relationships, often leading to conflicts, misunderstandings and a breakdown of trust (Not that you really care you fucken addict). Also, the stress that is associated with constantly thinking about gambling leads to anxiety, depression and other mental health issues. You will start failing in other departments of life.

Debt & Deceit

September-February 2023-24, peak period in terms of gambling, my bank statement during that time will leave you on the floor, about +R13,000 dedicated to gambling during that period. Yeah, I laugh about it now but man what the fuck, I was only 19, first job after high school. I'd often gamble a certain portion of my pay including half of my transport and lunch money, then make loans from friends and family, lie about how I used my money and all that. Well, you know how we addicts are I'd then gamble with the money borrowed, lose it and make more loans. I was stuck in a debt spiral. *Dikoloto after dikoloto jioh.*

Long story short, I didn't enjoy my money nor acquired any tangible material likes accessories and all that, it was just clothes and sneakers here and there. No contribution at home whatsoever. It came to a point whereby my income didn't even cover my debt, had to stall some people to give me time. I even had to quit my job because I didn't have transport money.

There's a slow, insidious crawl that happens when addiction takes hold. It doesn't come with a bang; it enters like a shadow, creeping up inch by inch, until it's all-encompassing. But once it's in? it has a very clear agenda; it wants everything you have, your time, energy, sanity and yes, your money. It's a reality many addicts face, the toll it takes on your financial-being, and the lies you tell others to justify it all. It doesn't start with a loan from someone, it starts much smaller than that, a tiny promise—like "let me dip into rent money, I'll replace it".

If you see yourself reaching the extent of borrowing money or using money saved for other things to gamble then it's essential to seek help and take action before it escalates. When you start asking people for money whether it's for something you say you need or for a certain emergency you lie about, you're now leveraging the trust people have in you, and that's when things get ugly. The first time you ask for a small loan from them, a little bit of cash to "cover an emergency", it won't feel like a betrayal at first, you'll convince yourself it's temporary you'll pay them back. You're now manipulating the situation to get what you really want: money to gamble. It will start small yeah, a one or two-hundred loan or maybe a voucher for gas or food, so you can use your own money to gamble. And they will trust you, feel sorry for you and give you. So, you ask, they give, and in that moment, you convince yourself it'll work, but it doesn't, it never does.

You'll always lie to them every time you ask for money, the problem is the more you lie, the more convincing you have to be. You start making up new stories, new explanations for why you need it. There's comfort in the deceit, because it gives you something to hold onto while everything else unravels. You can feel like you're still in control, even when it's clear you're not, saying things like "my next income, I'll clear all my debts and quit gambling". It's this deceit that grows the debt. You evens start resenting them for questioning you, because you're so convinced in your skull-petty sized head that you'll be just fine if they just gave you the money and stop asking questions. And the truth is the deeper you sink into this debt and deceit spiral, the more difficult it becomes to keep up the act. The lies become harder to sustain, and the cracks begin to show (well not for everyone, people are so good at it out there hey). But maybe they start noticing that your "emergencies" happen more often or start seeing through your excuses, every time the phone is in your hand you're panicking and don't want no one to see what you're doing.

Money will be lost, debts will be made—you'll find out that paying them off might just be the hardest things to do, friendship are now strained, maybe you even sell valuable things. Gambling addiction when you start making debts and lying about it will strip you of almost everything you hold dear until there's nothing left to take, it will take your self-worth, time, and eventually your dignity and that's when you realize that the debt isn't just financial anymore, it isn't the one that shows up in your inbox or haunts you with phone calls. It's the emotional debt—the one you owe the version of yourself that still believes it's possible to turn this around.

What you also don't realize is that the more you lie about it, the more isolated you become. You start pushing people away because you're afraid of them finding out, knowing the ugly truth—that you've been gambling away your money. But deep down you know that each lie makes it harder to come back, you know that every rand you beg for—whether it's for family or friends—drains your relationship with them bit by bit. You start to feel like a fraud, a total fuck-up, parasite leeching from the people who love and care about you. And instead of facing that, you make more debts, convincing yourself that if you just get the next win, you can pay them all back. But it's all a mirage and you know it.

At some point, the lies and debts will pile up. They always do. There won't be a way to gamble your way out of it. The only way is to win is to recognize that behavior as soon as you want to take a loan to gamble and face the truth, stop gambling or take a break. Reaching the extent to borrowing money to gamble and lying about is a major red flag, that's when you know you're already on the verge of being addicted or already are addicted.

Gambling addiction is never as simple as just craving something. It's about everything else it ruins in the process—the lies, the schemes, the debts, the desperate attempt to keep it under control, even as the weight of it drags you further under. It forces you to twist reality, reshape facts and often borrow from a future you haven't seen yet. Overall, it's a massive bank robbery, only the thief is you and the vault is your life.

Increase In Bets

One of the most significant red flags of the shift of recreational gambling to the onset of addiction is the moment a person begins to increase their bets. This is the most critical stage in the gambling process and often marks the beginning of a dangerous downward spiral. The moment you start raising your stakes, it can be after a series of losses, wins or it can be an increase in income or some, you're now stepping into a risky territory that can lead to a full-blown gambling addiction and chances are you might never lower your stakes anymore because it won't be enough for you, even small wins you used to cherish will never do for you anymore.

But one of the most common patterns it's when someone experiences a string of losses. In the moment it can feel incredibly frustrating and disheartening to lose over again and over again, so now the desire to "win it all back" becomes overwhelming. It's here the temptation to increase the size of your deposits/bets begins. This mindset, driven by the hope of a quick fix, is where many individuals begin to fall into the trap. The urge to place higher bets is not about enjoying the game or seeking the thrill but rather about chasing losses or desperate for a big win. Psychologically, this is a dangerous pattern that can feed into a vicious cycle. The more someone gets desperate for a big win whilst gambling or chase their losses, the greater the likelihood that they will lose more money, prompting them to bet even higher amounts in a desperate attempt to break even.

This behavior creates a destructive loop. The key issue here is the emotional compulsion that overrides rational thinking. At this stage, you're no longer gambling to win or for enjoyment; you are gambling because you kind-of feel the need to, you're drive by the desperation rather than the game itself. The psychological drive to increase bets, especially after losses or small wins, is deeply rooted in the brain's reward system. The anticipation of winning and the desire to achieve a sense of control can trigger the release of dopamine, that feel-good neurotransmitter and for those who are prone to addiction, this biochemical response can become reinforcing, making it difficult to stop gambling even in the face of significant losses or wins. When a person raises their bets, there is often an underlying belief that they can "beat the odds". They might convince themselves that the odds will eventually favor them, or that they are simply due for a win. This belief in luck or a change in fortune fuels the drive to place even larger bet amounts. However, the reality is that this behavior is rooted in a cognitive bias known as the "gambler's fallacy"—the false belief that previous outcomes influence future results in gambling. It's the standard dogma for most gamblers.

As bets increase, so do the stakes—financially, emotionally and psychologically. The moment someone begins to increase their bets, their financial situation may begin to suffer as a result, leading them to borrow money and start dipping into savings to continue gambling. The very same Archie Karas lost all his money due to increased bets because he felt he had enough money now and to make matters worse was the fact that he lost some of it, so to get it back is to increase more than he increased, and you know how the story goes. Unfortunately, the escalation is not limited to just money. The emotional and psychological toll starts to take over it's toll as well. Guilt, regret, shame and stress begin to accumulate as the person struggles to maintain control. At the same time, there is often a sense of denial about the severity of the problem, on some "blah blah blah to make money you have to use more money and take risk" philosophy bs. Many gamblers believe that if they just win once from recognizing that they are already deep in the grip of addiction.

What started as an occasional wager on a game or a single bet here and there can quickly evolve into a serious problem. When you become accustomed to increasing bets more than you can afford to lose, you can lose track of your financial reality, leading to a major financial strain. The more you increase your bets In an effort to "win it back" or "win huge", the deeper you descend into the addictive cycle. At this stage, the behavior no longer feels like a choice—-it feels like an uncontrollable urge, one that cannot be easily stopped hey. And here's the truth—this behavior will continue to grow because it's reinforced by intermittent wins, huge wins and you are less likely to lower your bets going forward. Even if they lose more often than they win, the occasional win with that high wager you put provides a momentary of rush of excitement and reinforces the belief that future success is just around the corner.

It's crucial to recognize when increasing bets has crossed the line into addiction, if you find yourself placing higher and higher bets in an attempt to achieve a higher win or recover previous losses, it may be the best time to step back and reevaluate your relationship with gambling. Just self-exclude man. And if you're gambling digitally it might be best you set a limit on your banking app.

The Lies We Tell Ourselves (The First Step to Overcoming Addiction Is Acknowledging Denial)

What I'm about to say isn't some fluffy, feel-good philosophy about "finding your inner peace", "embracing your truth" or any of that bullshit. Nope. This isn't a TED Talk where I serenade you with warm, fuzzy words and motivational quotes to make you feel all empowered for 10 minutes. What we're talking about in this sub-chapter is something far more uncomfortable, something that most people would rather avoid than confront. So thus isn't a sub-chapter full of "positive affirmations", it's a wake-up call, a punch in the gut that's going to make you squirm a little, but ultimately, it's the only way you're going to escape the trap you're fucken stuck in.

It starts with a whisper, a subtle lie "I've got this under control" "it's just a phase" "I can stop anytime I want" "Me addicted? Never, no ways". These are the lies we tell ourselves when we're trapped in the vicious cycle of addiction. But what we fail to realize those moments is that denial is not just a wall we build to protect ourselves from the harsh truth—it's a prison. A prison that keeps us from breaking free, and the first step to breaking free is acknowledging that we've been lying to ourselves.

Denial is often the first defense we put up when we confront the reality of gambling addiction or any other addiction. It's easier to believe the lie than to face the truth. Gambling addiction doesn't announce itself with a loud crash, it sneaks in, almost unnoticed, whispering small assurances that all is well. Denial is the lens through which addiction deceives us. When we believe that we can control our behavior, even as it spirals out of control, we distance ourselves from the destructive nature of our actions. It's estimated that 2-3% of the population experiences some form of gambling addiction, with a significant portion of these individuals unaware of the grip addiction has on them. Gambling addiction is the silent destroyer—it doesn't shout for attention; it whispers in the ear of it's victim, promising easy riches, and convincing them to keep playing just one more game, one more bet. It's like your drunkards friends at your birthday party offering you "just one more shot", even though you can barely stand and already on blackout. In fact, National Council on Problem Gambling estimates that about one in five problem gamblers will develop a severe gambling addiction. Even more telling up to 60% of gambling addicts have been reported to also suffer from depression, anxiety and other mental health issues. I used to have what we call "crash-outs". It's clear that the toll of gambling addiction is far-reaching, not just financially, but emotionally and psychologically as well.

It's important to understand why gambling addiction is considered one of the most dangerous forms of dependency. Unlike substances such as alcohol or drugs, gambling offers no immediate physical effects. There are no withdrawal symptoms, no obvious signs that the person is spiraling into destruction. But the damage is psychological, emotional and social. As the gamblers sinks deeper into the addiction, their need to chase that elusive high—the "win" that never comes—becomes more urgent. They begin to risk everything: relationships, careers, health and even their lives. "The craving to gamble is not based on reason or logic—it's a deep psychological need. The addict believes that the next bet, the next spin, the next hand of cards, will be the one that makes everything right." Dr. Robert Custer, a pioneer in addiction psychiatry. He also mentioned that a gambler can't avoid temptation even in a detox program or sober living facility because the temptation is everywhere. It's like someone put a Krispy Kreme donut shop on every street corner when you're trying to lose weight. Take the story of Emily, a woman in her 30s, whose life seemed perfect and eventually lost it all, it was only when she hit rock bottom—losing her job and almost her marriage—that she realized she had to face the truth. Her story is one of millions. Gambling is a pervasive, destructive force that leaves individuals feeling trapped and powerless. It's often said that gambling addiction is the addiction that doesn't look like an addiction. The external signs aren't immediately apparent, but the internal devastation is often catastrophic.

Behind every number is a person, a family, a life torn apart by the invisible shackles of addiction. Consider Relebogile Tsotetsi, a mother of two, whom at 35 had lost everything. I don't normally do this because my experience with gambling it's of a teenager and I believe most readers here will be friends and acquaintances, even family and if some are gambling addicts it's not to that extent like the story I'm about to tell but the truth is it might get there without any realization so it's important to tell. And also, it's through stories, someone else's experiences and histories we learn. And please don't give me the "it will never happen to me" bullshit, be careful who you look down upon and wish to avoid becoming. Rele's descent into casino after work to "de-stress". A fun activity to unwind after a long day, but it quickly spiraled out of control. What started as entertainment soon morphed into obsession. It became a thing of her spending more and more of her paychecks at the casino, telling herself it's all just for fun. Within two years apparently, she had maxed out her credit cards, borrowed money from friends, and dipped into her children's savings. She even pawned her engagement ring to fund her next gambling session. "I'll win it all back" "I still have time to quit and start saving again" she kept telling herself. But instead, her life unraveled. Her children barely recognized her anymore, as she'd get home seeing everything wrong and throwing tantrums, her husband filed for divorce. Relebogile's story isn't unique, it's just one of many stories of people who believed the lie for far too long and paid the price. The financial toll of gambling addiction is staggering (in Peter Drury's voice) According to *Psychology Today*, the average debt for someone with a gambling addiction is $55,000 in the US, and for those who struggle with severe gambling problems, the debt can easily exceed $100,000. But the cost goes beyond money. The cruel irony is unlike other addictions, the thrill of the game isn't merely about the money—it's about the money—it's about the hope, the belief that one more bet, one more game, will change everything. But for most gamblers, that "change" never comes.

The journey to recovery begins with a moment of clarity. A moment when we finally look in the mirror and confront the lies we've been telling ourselves. "I'm not really an addict" "I don't need help", "I can just quit anytime" These lies are insidious because they give us a false sense of control and keep us from getting the help we need. It's like trying to quit smoking by saying, "I'll just finish this bag/box, then I'll be done for good" we all know how that ends. And even if you quit, you're more likely to relapse with "one more joint/cigarette because I feel happy and I've quit". Watching a movie like *The wolf of wall street* or any other empowering gambling-related film can also easily trigger a shift in your mindset, making you start to believe that gambling is where you truly belong. It creates this illusion that you can be the mastermind of something, you get swept into the idea of power, wealth, and success, and before you know it, you're facing an identity crisis where it feels impossible to walk away. It's like the more you see it, the more your brain convinces you that you should be that person. It's crazy how the mind plays tricks on us, making us think we're meant for something that's not even real. Real-world data backs up the approach of admitting when you're powerless, according to the *Gambling Therapy Project*. I don't really recommend treatment programs because I've never done one. Individuals who enters support programs are more likely to recover, with 40-60% of gamblers improving after joining a treatment program, the crucial point here is that acknowledgement of the problem is always the first step but never the last because I know friends who I engage in "parlay builds" who'd often say "I'm addicted, I have to quit this but I gotta make some more for this and that" "I love the game, I love hustle" bs, and I don't think that means they're "really" admitting fully, because they think as though they still stand a chance in the game of chance. Though admitting is still the hardest step. Once you've broken the wall of denial, the path to recovery becomes clearer. Overcoming addiction requires more than just recognizing the problem—it requires active engagement and commitment.

So, recognizing and addressing addiction is paramount. It's crucial to understand the signs and symptoms of gambling addiction, such as a preoccupation with gambling. interfering with your personal life also increasing bets to achieve desired excitement, lying about gambling habits and reaching the extent of borrowing money to gamble. If you find yourself experiencing these behaviors, it's essential to seek immediate help and take action before it escalates. Remember, gambling should be an enjoyable past time, not a destructive habit. Prioritize responsible gambling practices, set limits for yourself and seek support if you feel your gambling habits are getting out of control. Self-exclude from your betting accounts, install a software that blocks all gambling sites. Download apps like Streaks to track your progress, it is said that streaks make habits easy as you get to celebrate small milestones. Your well-being is priceless and seeking help early can prevent further harm. Gambling addiction as I've explained is often considered the most severe addiction due to the devastating impact it has. Stats revealed it's staggering toll. It's associated with higher rates of bankruptcy, huge chunk of debts, divorce and suicide than any other addiction.

Don't make the mistake of telling yourself you are in control, don't lie to yourself, believe you me YOU ARE NOT. Admitting powerlessness is the first step towards liberation. Embrace this truth and break free from the chains of denial and reclaim your life whilst there's still time.

ENDGAME

No One Is Crazy

Fuuucken hell. I can't even tell you how good it feels to finally get to this point. It's like building up to the climax of a story that's been unfolding in the back of my mind for years and I don't even know what the fuck this sub-chapter is really all about, but it doesn't mean I'm crazy for wanting to write it, I know what I'm doing but in a much more real sense I have no idea what I'm doing.

So, no one is crazy, everybody knows what they're doing. People do some dumb shit in life, people gamble their whole life savings, people gamble with their homes, cars, people will bet a team with 00000.001 odds of winning, these are some crazy things people do in gambling, but no one is crazy, everybody knows what they're doing. Everyone has their own view and experiences on how gambling or the world really works. What seems crazy to you might actually make sense to them. The gambler betting on Southampton to beat Man City knows what he's doing. You know what pisses me off? When people tell you you're crazy for making a big decision, for taking a big risk It's almost like the moment you step outside of the comfort zone of the "normal" path, the standard dogma, then everybody decides that you've lost your mind. Real success, growth and change—all comes from making decisions that looks reckless as hell to the outside world. Take Steve Jobs for example, dropped out of college and took risks that were kind of reckless but ended up shaping Apple. His journey wasn't linear nor clean, but in the middle of that chaos he knew what he was doing. This example yeah, yeah, I know it's far-fetched considering we talking about gambling but my chat is everybody knows what they're doing, no one's crazy. And I don't know about you, but I'm not here for some safe, boring life. I'm here for calculated chaos, taking risks, for betting on myself. And yeah, I know that this sub-chapter is going to be a gamble.

Look, when I decided to write this book, I could've easily played it safe. I could've removed all the profanity, softened my tone, and aimed at a bigger audience. But when I made a decision to add vulgarity, I knew it was going to limit the market as it might become 18+ rated, and that could reduce my potential readers by a significant amount. It would shrink the pool, but the thing is I didn't care, I knew exactly what I was doing, it wasn't about the rands or the numbers. It was about staying authentic to what it's supposed to be, expressing how I really felt writing all this, when I gamble and all that. Real, unfiltered and raw. I didn't want to be another self-help book that's just floating around with generic advice. And people will think you're crazy for doing things like that. People don't get your choices because they don't have your context.

Gambling simply magnifies the odds and stakes. It distills life into pure form. No one questions whether it's rational to rent a house or take a loan for education, even though these are far riskier decisions that can shape our future. Why? Because the randomness and uncertainty are hidden beneath layers of social validation and conventionality. But when we sit a poker table, place a bet on a team, horse or roll the dice to alter our circumstances, the randomness becomes painfully visible. And that's why it feels and looks "crazy". Our bets expose us to the rawness of uncertainty—and who wants to face that? We're all in the same boat. Cognitive dissonance is a powerful force.

It's the internal battle that occurs when our beliefs don't align with our behaviors, and it explains why gamblers often appear irrational. Imagine a man who has lost thousands in a casino, but still convinces himself that the next hand will be different and it's due for a win. He believes deeply, that his luck is about to turn, this belief is not madness, well it is but hear me out, it's not, it's the mind's way of reconciling loss with hope. We do this everyday in different areas of life. Every time we buy a product, we're given reasons to justify the purchase, even if we can't afford it. Every time we tell ourselves we'll start a diet tomorrow, we're denying the obvious reality that we've failed in the past. This need to avoid cognitive dissonance keeps us tethered to irrational beliefs—and gambling is no different. The gambler's mind creates stories to make sense of madness, telling itself "I'm due for a win". This is the very same delusion that keeps us clinging to the idea that a failed relationship will work out if we just try harder or that a poor investment will rebound if we give it more time.

No one's crazy for gambling—it's not irrationality; it's the desire to be part of something larger.

Greed (Through Two Stories, Two Men, One Gamble)

VICTOR HADLEY didn't need any more money. He had millions stacked up in accounts all over the world. Born into an old-money family, he had inherited his father's wealth. If money was the game, he had already won. A multi-millionaire, owner of several massive companies. But his eyes were still burned with hunger, a hunger that couldn't be satisfied. The numbers on his bank account only seemed to grow, yet they felt hollow. He is spending his life trying to keep up with the billionaires—their endless parties with top politicians, their jets, their sprawling estates. I guess you'd say he wanted respect, the kind you get that comes from being the biggest name in the room. It had been the early 2000s when he started to feel the gnawing emptiness of his fortune. The internet boom had created a new breed of wealth—young, brash and brimming with self-made billionaires who had skyrocketed to fame overnight. He was a product of inheritance rather than innovation, he had money yes but nothing new to offer and so he found himself competing with those around him, constantly trying to keep up but failing. It was until the 2007-08 great recession, most of his companies collapsed, triggered by the housing market crash and the subsequent credit crisis, so it was a step-back. He still did okay, some of his companies survived but he wasn't rich like before. The catalyst came when he heard the story of a former tech millionaire, now a self-styled venture capitalist, who had turned his life around after a series of high-stakes gambles in the world of poker and private casino games. Victor's obsession grew— "if someone like him could turn a few millions into a billion, then why couldn't I? I have the connections and money" he said. The Blue Crescent Casino—an exclusive establishment built for the ultra-wealthy had just opened, and Victor couldn't resist. Every night after his meetings he'd head there. Victor wasn't interested in winning for the sake of money, because the truth is on paper he had money, enough despite losing most of it during the recession. It wasn't even the trill of the gamble either—it was about the story he wanted to be able to say he was the man who gambled it all and came out on top and recovered all the wealth he lost during the recession. It was the narrative of triumph, being one of the richest in the world. But the more he played, the more he risked. He had always been a man who calculated risk—he understood the market, knew how to manage wealth, but in the casino there was no market, no predictability, no formulas. It was just chance. All to keep up with the Johannson's or any other billionaires out there. His losses mounted—millions lost in a single night, his companies all collapsed and he was in a much bigger debt he could imagine. Now owing millions in taxes, to corporates and all that.

TOMMY RIVAS on the other hand, had been in and out of jobs since the age of 16. Raised in a small, neglected apartment in a run-down neighborhood, he never really had a shot at the good life. He worked two dead-end jobs, one as a dishwasher at a local diner and another as a security guard at a run-of-the-mill shopping center. His life was a routine of waking up early, working long hours and barely making ends meet. Every month was one step away from being homeless. But despite the struggle, he had a dream: a better life man. His wife also two scrappy jobs, leaving their daughter to fend for herself much more than she should have. Tommy would often gamble on lottery tickets, with no luck he decided to play slots machines just for the thrill of it and maybe he might stand a chance. He would often win few hundred rands here and there. He would then go and bet larger amount and win at time, his initial success was a drug, he won small amounts, and it gave him hope—real, burning hope—that could change everything and alter his circumstances. Maybe, just maybe a bigger win could pull him out of the cycle of poverty. He spent nights at the casino, slot sides, each one more night desperate than the last. The more he won, the more he began to believe that this was the only way to escape his circumstances. But with every win the stakes grew. His winnings became an illusion for success, and his losses—an all-consuming fear. The promise of a better life became a weight too heavy to carry. He was no longer gambling to make money for bread, there was more to him than meets the eye. One night he went all out, all his income, rent money and even sold the car that was just about to break down. Guess what? The inevitable happened, he lost everything, in the span of a few hours. Tommy sat at the ringing slot machine, his hands shaking as he realized the truth—he had gambled his own hope, and now it has evaporated.

THE KEY TAKEAWAY here is that Victor and Tommy stories diverge in their motivations, but they are united by one core element; the desire for something more. For Victor, to prove he's the best in a world of billionaires—insatiable need for recognition, status and validation. For Tommy, it's the desperate hope of escaping poverty, providing a better life for his family. Yet, despite their differing circumstances and social classes, both are driven by the same destructive force, GREED.

Victor's greed is driven by vanity—the need to be seen as someone who matters in the highest echelons of society, a deep seated for power, control. His wealth is not enough, for the fact that he lost most of it makes matters worse. But in his blind pursuit of status, he risks everything, including his sanity.

Tommy's greed, however is born of desperation. He gambles for hope, he seeks escape from poverty, not glory. But his desperation blinds him to the true cost of his choices, losing the little he had, his situation being worse.

When associated with gambling, greed can escalate, whether rich or poor. It's a common human trait, it's innate in humans. It's something that resides within all of us, particularly surfaces in financial pursuits. When money is on the table, it has a way of captivating our minds. It beckons, it calls, and suddenly we believe there is more to be had. We get wrapped up in the idea of more—more and more. For the wealthy, it often manifests in an insatiable desire to accumulate more wealth, not necessary out of need, but for the sake of power, status, or even the thrill of acquisition. Take the story of Bernie Madoff for instance, he built an empire worth millions, doing well but it wasn't enough until he had to now create a Ponzi scheme to accumulate more and take more from people. For the poor, it often comes from the place of desperation and survival, they desire to attain what they do not have—simply a better life or keeping up with *Makhi*—fuels their greed. So, in his context, it's a way to escape from their circumstances or an obsession with acquiring resources that seems out of reach.

Unfortunately, this often leads to unhealthy patterns and as you saw how Victor and Tommy ended up by now you must know that in gambling, greed ultimately proves to be dangerous.

So, my chat is gambling doesn't matter what your social-economic class is, rich or poor, we all playing the same game. You might go to the tables to win money for bread or to make ends meet, but before you know it, you're caught in the rush, seeing yourself with hundreds of thousands, losing sight of the bigger picture. On the other hand, you might sit at the table just for fun, because you're rich and looking for a thrill, but suddenly, you find yourself chasing the same level as Jeff Bezos or Elon Musk, wanting to reach their income class, blinded by the lure of more and more. As Gamblers, we often don't see each other the same way. For example, someone playing roulette, losing 20K a round might feel like the people on the same round as them losing 50 rands a round seems insignificant. But don't understand what the R50 means to them—it's their pocket money, the last they have. So is the same as the person betting those R50 seeing someone betting 20K's feels like life is not fair, someone is betting money I don't even dream of winning in that particular round. Greed blinds us to our different realities, making it hard to truly understand what the person is going through.

Greed is a powerful and often destructive force, manifesting in unique ways, yet its effects are universal, shaping lives, behaviors, and even societies.

JUST DON'T GET GREEDY.

The Final Spin

AS THE FINAL CHAPTER closes, and you turn your final pages, remember that the game is never truly over. The strategies you've learned, the techniques you've mastered, and the discipline you've cultivated are just the beginning of a new approach to gambling and to life. The odds may never be fully in your favor, but armed with this playbook, you now have the power to tilt them in your direction.

I hope this journey has taught you more than just how to gamble—but also shown you how to think, how to act and control the impulses that often drive us to recklessness. It's about playing with purpose, not just for the thrill. Each decision you make is an opportunity to solidify your place in this game, not as a mere participant, but as the master of the rules you create. True gambling mastery comes when you understand that winning isn't just about the payoff, but about knowing your limits, managing your money and most importantly, understanding the profound impact of self-discipline. As you move forward remember that success in gambling is a marathon, not a sprint. The tools you've gained here will serve you not just in the casino, but in all aspects of your life, more especially financially. Life itself is a game of strategy, and the principle of smart gambling—focus, patience, discipline—are the same that will lead you to triumph in any endeavor. The game may be unpredictable, but the true victory lies in your ability to rewrite the rules, to chart your own course, and to consistently make intelligent, informed decisions. The final spin is yours, but it's not just about what happens next—it's about how you play the rest of the game. So, step forward, knowing that with wisdom and strategy, you are now the one in control.

But beyond the strategies and technique lies a deeper truth, the greatest gamble is the one we take on ourselves. It is the journey of self-discovery, the test of resilience, and the quest for balance. In the pursuit of fortune, may you find not only riches but also wisdom, not only success but also humility. So, as you step into the labyrinth of uncertainty, remember that the true prize is not always found in the pot at the end of the rainbow but in the journey itself.

May this playbook not only be a tool for triumph but also a companion in your quest for self-mastery. With each wager, may you bet not just with your chips but with your character, for in the end, it is not the cards you hold but the person you become that truly matters. With that, I bid you farewell on your odyssey through the exhilarating realm of gambling. May your decision be smart, your resolve unyielding and your journey filled with moments of both triumph and introspection. Best of luck at the tables, dear gambler, as you embark on this timeless adventure. And remember in the game of life, may your greatest gamble always be on yourself.

A-a-a-a-and then we were done,

I started writing this book feeling like a total deadbeat—like I wasn't really doing anything with purpose. But along the way, something shifted. It's been grind—late nights, constantly watching the clock, laptop on my feet, notepad and pen always within reach. Meditating, reading, hitting the gym—just trying to find balance. It felt good, but after a while, it started to feel boring, too much pressure, same routine. But I was much more fulfilled, I guess that's where the growth happens, right? In the quiet, steady grind, having some sense of direction. It's not flashy but it's real.

This book might not do what I hope, but I guess we'll never know unless I put it out there. It wasn't about chasing success nor money—it was about getting my work out there and enriching whatever's left in the process. I'm not really an author—I'm just someone with a story, few tips, and the newly-grown love for writing, learning from best self-help selling authors books I read and the courage to gamble on putting all this together. Without gambling, there's no book, that's the truth.

And right now, after those 9 hours a day dedicated to it, all those headaches of it not coming together. I feel like Thanos after he wiped the entire universe (no pun intended). I'm just sitting there, watching the sunset on a beautiful, new world. The work is done, the game is played. No more long hours of my fingers cramping, mind blowing. Just a quiet sense of knowing that it's all out there, and it was worth the risk.

So, how will the book do? Hard to say, maybe it will connect with readers, maybe it won't. I guess I'll never know now. As for another book? I can't see it, like I said I'm not a seasoned author, I don't even know what it will be about or why I'd bother but there is a danger that is associated with pure certainty, I can't be sure. Maybe there will be another book, or maybe not. I guess I'll never know now.

Last chapter that I do, feels like surgery. Takin' years off from all this, I need recovery. So, maybe getting back to my regular life will humble me. I'll be back 2026 to share the aftermath.

More Life.

ACKNOWLEDGEMENTS

I am deeply indebted to the individuals whose unwavering support and encouragement helped elevate the quality of the book, transforming my scrappy collections on gambling tips into a polished and insightful guide book, surpassing its humble beginnings.

To those who championed my work from its earliest stages, offering praise and encouragement as I shared snippets and quotes from its draft form, your words of affirmation were a beacon of light on this creative journey

A heartfelt thank you to my former manager and life coach at Man Trucks and Bus, Jurie De Winaar, whose belief in my potential inspired me to take the leap and share it with the world, despite seeing only a glimpse of this project.

Your words, have been instrumental in bringing this project to fruition, urging me not to keep it hidden but to trust in its potential and get it out there.

To my dear family friend, Mr. Karabo Tsiri, your counsel and unwavering support have been a constant source of strength. Your reminders to be patient, to allow the ideas to evolve naturally, and to trust in the process have been invaluable as i navigated the challenges of writing and publication

I extend my heartfelt gratitude to my friends Keotshepile Maluleka, Refentse Matseke and Lethabo Kgobe for the invaluable assistance.

Keotshepile helped with the research on publishing processes and platforms. Refentse, for being there when I needed guidance and reassurance. whilst Lethabo provided additional editing support on my previous first edition, refining my work and probably the voice behind my upcoming audiobook of this book. Your dedication and expertise have been pivotal in shaping this book into its final form.

I am also immensely grateful to Rearabetswe Mokwena for bringing my vision for the cover to life with creativity and skill. Your collaboration added depth and resonance to the final product, and I want to extend my thanks to you for your talent

To all those who offered feedback, shared encouragement, and believed in this project, thank you for your support. This book is a testament to the power collaboration and community, and I am honored to share it with you.

All thanks to my addiction, for being the driving force behind the creation of " THE COMPLETE GAMBLING PLAYBOOK ". It might seem unconventional, but it played a significant role in sparking the idea for this book. Confronting my addiction changed everything, it droved me deeper into the world of gambling, inspiring me to share my knowledge

And finally, to my MOM & DAD, Thank You For EVERYTHING!

ABOUT THE AUTHOR

JUST A KID FROM SKRAAL...

Meet Amogelang Herman Legwabe, a spirited individual born on July

28th, 2004, proudly hailing from the vibrant city of Pretoria, South Africa. Despite his tender age of 19, Amogelang's roots run deep, tracing back to the lively hometown of Hammanskraal, close-knit community of TEMBA

Though not initially a seasoned author, his journey into the realm of literature was ignited by an unexpected source – his own struggles with gambling. Who found himself entangled in the web of bad gambling habits. But instead of succumbing to its grasp, he turned the tables, using his experiences as fuel for a remarkable endeavor. Thus, from the ashes of his trials emerged a bold and unconventional idea – "The Complete Gambling Playbook."

So, dear reader, as you reach the conclusion of this captivating tome, remember that behind every word lies a story, and behind every story, a storyteller. And in this case, that storyteller is none other than the indomitable Amogelang Herman Legwabe, mfana wase kasi – a name poised to leave an indelible mark on the literary landscape.

THE COMPLETE GAMBLING PLAYBOOK 21

Definitions to help

(in order of chapters)

1. Pulsate: to expand and contract rhythmically
2. Lure: to tempt into a trap
3. Peril: an immediate danger
4. Treacherous: Dangerous
5. Turmoil: wild confusion or agitation
6. Folly: Lack of good sense;foolishness
7. Essence: most important quality or element of something
8. Paradox: Statement, situation that seems contradictory but upon closer look/examination reveals hidden truth or logical possibility
9. Orchestrate: to coordinate carefully
10. Fray: to become ragged with loose threads
11. Ignite: To set fire to
12. Culminate: to reach the highest or last point
13. Intricate: very complicated
14. Abyss: an extremely deep pit
15. Introspection: examining your own thoughts and feelings
16. Fugazi: Slang used for false, bogus, inauthentic
17. Beckon: to make a sign to a person to come
18. Prevail: to be the most frequent or general
19. Fluctuate: to rise and fall
20. Improbable: unlikely
21. Odyssey: a long adventurous journey
22. Slippery slope: A course of action likely to lead to something bad or disastrous.
23. Slippery slope fallacy: An argument that claims an initial event or action will trigger series of events and lead to an undesirable outcome

24. Exhilarate: To make someone happy and excited.

CREDITS

—-

Author:

Amogelang Herman Mkhonza

Editors:

Amogelang Herman Mkhonza

Cover Design:

Rearabetswe Mokwena

Amogelang Herman Mkhonza

About the Author

JUST A KID FROM SKRAAL...

Meet Amogelang Herman Legwabe , a spirited individual born on July 28th, 2004, proudly hailing from the vibrant city of Pretoria, South Africa. Despite his tender age of 19, Amogelang's roots run deep, tracing back to the lively hometown of Hammanskraal , close-knit community of TEMBA

Though not initially a seasoned author, his journey into the realm of literature was ignited by an unexpected source – his own struggles with gambling. Yes, you heard it right. Amogelang, just a kid from Skraal, found himself entangled in the web of bad gambling habits. But instead of succumbing to its grasp, he turned the tables, using his experiences as fuel for a remarkable endeavor. Thus, from the ashes of his trials emerged a bold and unconventional idea – The Complete Gambling Playbook.

So, dear reader, as you reach the conclusion of this captivating tome, remember that behind every word lies a story, and behind every story, a storyteller. And in this case, that storyteller is none other than the indomitable Amogelang Herman Legwabe – a name poised to leave an indelible mark on the literary landscape.

www.ingramcontent.com/pod-product-compliance
Lightning Source LLC
LaVergne TN
LVHW090424210926
848480LV00002B/682
* 9 7 9 8 2 3 0 0 3 8 6 7 2 *